WHAT IS
the Relationship
between CHURCH
and STATE?

The Crucial Questions Series By R.C. Sproul

Who Is Jesus?

Can I Trust the Bible?

Does Prayer Change Things?

Can I Know God's Will?

How Should I Live in This World?

What Does It Mean to Be Born Again?

Can I Be Sure I'm Saved?

What Is Faith?

What Can I Do with My Guilt?

What Is the Trinity?

What Is Baptism?

Can I Have Joy in My Life?

Who Is the Holy Spirit?

Does God Control Everything?

How Can I Develop a Christian Conscience?

What Is the Lord's Supper?

What Is the Church?

What Is Repentance?

What Is the Relationship between Church and State?

Are These the Last Days?

What Is the Great Commission?

Can I Lose My Salvation?

Free digital editions available at ReformationTrust.com/FreeCQ

CRUCIAL
QUESTIONS
No. | 19

WHAT IS
the Relationship
between CHURCH
and STATE?

R.C. SPROUL

IR *Reformation Trust*   A DIVISION OF LIGONIER MINISTRIES, ORLANDO, FL

What Is the Relationship between Church and State?

© 2014 by R.C. Sproul

Published by Reformation Trust Publishing
A division of Ligonier Ministries
421 Ligonier Court, Sanford, FL 32771
Ligonier.org   ReformationTrust.com

Printed in North Mankato, MN
Corporate Graphics
October 2015
First edition, fifth printing

Cover design: Gearbox Studios
Interior design and typeset: Katherine Lloyd, The DESK

All Scripture quotations are from *The Holy Bible, English Standard Version*, copyright © 2001 by Crossway Bibles, a division of Good News Publishers. Used by permission. All rights reserved.

Library of Congress Cataloging-in-Publication Data

Sproul, R. C. (Robert Charles), 1939-
  What is the relationship between church and state? / by R.C. Sproul.
    pages cm. -- (Crucial questions ; No. 19)
  ISBN 978-1-56769-374-4 -- ISBN 1-56769-374-1
1. Church and state. I. Title.
  BV630.3.S67 2014
  261.7--dc23

                                    2014006857

Contents

Chapter One

LEGAL FORCE

A few years ago, I was invited to be the keynote speaker at the inaugural prayer breakfast for the governor of Florida. At that breakfast, I addressed not only the group of people who were assembled, but also the governor himself. I said that the event was similar to an ordination service in a church. At an ordination service, a man is consecrated to the sacred ministry of the gospel and is set apart for that vocation in the church. I tried to impress upon the governor the weight of his office:

Today is your ordination day. Today is your ordination sermon, or ordination ceremony. Your office is ordained by God, just like mine is as a pastor. It is because of God's authority that there is such a thing as government. For this reason, you are called by God to be a minister, not as a preacher in a local church, but as an official of this state. However, in your office as governor, you are not given autonomous authority. Your authority, and the only authority that you have whatsoever, is an authority delegated to you by the One who possesses all authority, and that is God. Ultimately, God is the foundation of authority by which you will rule in government. I challenge you this day to always remember that you are accountable to God for how you exercise that office, and may you not be seduced by this mythological concept of separation of church and state. The state, as much as the church, is instituted by God, ordained by God, and derives whatever authority it has through the delegation of divine authority. The state, therefore, is answerable and accountable to God.

At that time, I was able to say this to the governor of our state. However, to speak in these terms today is to be a voice of one crying in the wilderness. We live in a society that has been radically secularized and where it's assumed that the civil government is not answerable to God and, in fact, has a right to be godless.

In the United States, we often hear the phrase *separation of church and state*, but it should be noted that this phrase does not occur in the country's founding documents. It is not found in the Declaration of Independence, the Constitution, or the Bill of Rights. It comes from a remark made by Thomas Jefferson about the principles that he believed were implied in the founding documents of the United States. But it has now become perhaps the only remaining absolute in American culture: the absolute principle of the absolute separation of church and state.

From the very beginning of Christianity, the relationship between church and state has been a matter of great concern. When we look at the Old Testament, we see that Israel was a theocracy, a state that was ruled by God through anointed kings. Though the church and state had certain distinctions—including distinctions between the work of priests (the church) and the work of kings (the state)—the two institutions were so closely integrated that to speak of separation of the two would be fallacious.

However, once the New Testament community was established, the church became a missionary church, reaching out to various nations, tribes, and peoples who were ruled by secular governments. Christians had to face the question of how they were to relate to the Roman Empire, to the magistrate in Corinth, or to the local authorities wherever the church spread. For centuries, the church has had to carefully examine its role in society—especially when that society does not officially hold to a Christian worldview. In order to understand the relationship between church and state from a biblical perspective, we must ask some fundamental questions.

There are many different types and structures of government, but what is the essence, the fundamental principle, of government? The answer to that question is one word: *force*. Government is force—but it's not just any kind of force. It's force that is supported by an official, legal structure. Government is a structure that is endowed legally with the right to use force to compel its citizens to do certain things and not do other things.

Some years ago, I had lunch with a well-known United States senator. We were discussing some of the issues involved with the Vietnam War—then being waged amid great controversy—when he said to me, "I don't believe that any government has the right to force its citizens to do what they don't want to do." I almost choked on my soup! I said to him: "Senator, what I hear you saying is that no government has the right to govern. If you take legal force away from government, it is then reduced to simply making suggestions. But isn't it true that when governments enact laws, the government functions as that which is designed to enforce whatever laws are enacted?"

Ultimately, the original form of government rests on the rule and authority of God Himself. God is the author of the universe, and with that authorship comes the authority over what He has made: "The earth is the LORD's and the fullness thereof" (Ps. 24:1).

We can see a form of government in the creation account. When God created human beings, He gave them a mission: "Be fruitful and multiply and fill the earth and subdue it, and have dominion over the fish of the sea and over the birds of the heavens and over every living thing that moves on the earth" (Gen. 1:28). Adam and Eve were to act as rulers in God's stead, as His vice-regents over creation. God delegated to Adam and Eve dominion over the earth, so that they were to exercise authority over the animals. It was not authority over people, but it was authority over the earth and the environs and the creatures therein, over all of the lesser forms of divine creation.

God also gave Adam and Eve a prohibition: they were not to eat of the Tree of Knowledge of Good and Evil. God gave an ominous warning of what would happen if they transgressed His command: "For in the day that you eat of it you shall surely die" (Gen. 2:17). This means that penal sanctions would be imposed by His authority. When Adam and Eve disobeyed His rule and rebelled against His authority, they did not immediately undergo physical death, but rather spiritual death. Physical death was postponed until later, as God in His graciousness exercised mercy. However, one of the punishments that He imposed upon these rebellious creatures was to banish them from the garden of Eden.

We next see a manifestation of earthly government in the angel that God placed at the entrance to the garden of Eden. The angel stood at the gateway to Eden with a flaming sword. The flaming sword functioned as an instrument of force to prevent Adam and Eve from returning to the paradise in which they had been placed.

The next issue we should consider is the purpose of government. Early in church history, Saint Augustine made the observation that government is a necessary evil, for in this world among fallen human creatures, you will never find a morally perfect government. All governments, no matter what structure they manifest, are representative of fallen humanity because governments are made up of sinful people. We all know that human government can be corrupt. Augustine's point was this: government itself is evil, but it's a necessary evil; it's necessary because evil in our world needs to be restrained. One means of this restraint is human government. In light of this, Augustine argued that human government was not necessary before the fall.

Thomas Aquinas disagreed with Augustine on this point. He still saw a role for government in managing the division of labor that one could imagine in a hypothetical unfallen creation. Thomas certainly agreed that the primary purpose of government was to restrain evil. To both Thomas and Augustine, the primary purpose for which government was instituted was to exercise restraint upon human evil and to preserve the very possibility of human existence. Therefore, the first task of government is to protect people from evil and to preserve and maintain human life.

Another role that government fulfills is protecting human property. Many people seek to violate other human beings by stealing, abusing, or destroying their property.

A final role for government is regulating agreements, upholding contracts, and ensuring just weights and balances. Government should seek to protect people from the injustice of fraud. The butcher who puts his thumb surreptitiously on the scale along with the meat that he is weighing has injured his customer by inflating the cost of the goods through a fraudulent practice. Government is necessary to regulate this behavior by devising just weights, measurements, and standards.

God created government in order to protect humanity—but not just humanity. Government is to protect the world itself as well. When Adam and Eve were placed in the magnificent garden, they were given the mandate from God to tend, till, and cultivate the garden. They knew they were not called to exploit or abuse this world. Therefore, governments, as a manifestation of man's call by God to be His vice-regents, have a role in regulating how we treat

God's creatures and creation—not just human beings, but also animals and the environment in which we live.

Such regulation is a good thing, but it is worth noting that even in its most benign form, government involves restrictions on people's liberty. We boast as Americans that we live in a free country, and that's true, relatively speaking; but no people in any land have ever lived in an atmosphere of complete freedom. Every law that is ever enacted by any legislative body restricts someone's freedom. If we enact a law against murder, we're placing restrictions on the criminal's right to kill a person with malice aforethought. Every single law that is passed restricts someone's freedom. Some freedoms are good to restrict—such as the freedom to murder—and others are not. This is why we have to be exceedingly careful every time we pass a law. We need to realize what we are doing. We need to remember that we are taking freedom away from people, and the longer we do that in a careless manner, the less liberty we are left with in our lives.

Clearly, the state has been instituted by God and we do have government. The question then becomes, How are we as Christians to relate to that government? That is the question we will seek to answer in the rest of this book.

Chapter Two

CIVIL
OBEDIENCE

Obeying authority is hard. We bristle anytime we
hear someone say: "You must do this. You ought to
do that." We want to be able to say: "Don't tell me what
to do. I want to do what *I* want to do." We want people
to empower and entitle us. We hate receiving mandates.
That's our nature.

In light of this, I like to talk about a Christian world-
view and how it differs from a pagan worldview. One way

to differentiate the two would be to consider each world-view's understanding of responsibility toward authority. If I were not a Christian, I certainly wouldn't embrace submission to authority. But being a Christian makes me hesitate before I live in active disobedience to those whom God has put in authority over me.

To understand why, we must look at the New Testament's explanation of the origin and function of government under God. This issue is clearly dealt with by the Apostle Paul in the thirteenth chapter of his epistle to the Romans.

Romans 13 begins: "Let every person be subject to the governing authorities. For there is no authority except from God, and those that exist have been instituted by God. Therefore whoever resists the authorities resists what God has appointed, and those who resist will incur judgment" (vv. 1–2). Paul begins this study of the government with an Apostolic command for everyone to submit to governing authorities. This lays a framework for Christian civil disobedience.

Paul's teaching in Romans 13:1–2 is not an isolated instance in the New Testament. Paul is simply reiterating here what he teaches elsewhere, what is also taught by Peter in his epistles—and by our Lord Himself—that there is a fundamental obligation of the Christian to be a model of civil obedience. We as the people of God are called upon to be as obedient as we possibly can in good conscience to the powers that be. Remember that Paul is writing this to people who are under the oppression of the Roman government. He's telling people to be submissive to a government that would eventually execute him. But he doesn't do so in a blind sense that precludes any possibility of civil disobedience.

For now, I want us to see that Paul is setting the stage in Romans 13 for explaining why the Christian is supposed to be particularly scrupulous and sensitive in civil obedience. Paul begins to set forth his case by saying, "Let every person be subject to the governing authorities." Why? "For there is no authority except from God." Peter puts it another way. He tells us to submit ourselves to the earthly authorities for the Lord's sake (1 Peter 2:13). That means that if I show no respect to a person whom God has set in authority between Himself and me, my disrespect carries beyond that person and ultimately lands on God as the giver of the authority.

The biblical concept of authority is hierarchical. At the top of the hierarchy is God. All authority rests ultimately in God, and there is no authority invested in any institution or in any person except through the delegation of that authority from God. Any authority that I have in any area of my life is a derived, appointed, and delegated authority. It is not intrinsic but extrinsic. It is given ultimately by the One who has inherent authority.

Within this hierarchy structure, God the Father gives all authority on heaven and earth to Christ, His Son (Matt. 28:18). God has enthroned Christ as the King of kings. So if Christ is the prime minister of the universe, it means that all the kings of this world have a King who reigns over them and that all the earthly lords have a superior Lord to whom they are accountable. We know that there are vast multitudes of people in this world who do not recognize Christ as their King, and because His kingdom is invisible right now, they say, "Where is this king? I don't see any reigning king." In light of this, the task of the church is of cosmic political proportions.

In Acts 1:8, Jesus gave a mandate to His disciples: "And you will be my witnesses in Jerusalem and in all Judea and Samaria, and to the end of the earth" (Acts 1:8). They were to be *witnesses,* but witnesses to what? The immediate context of this verse is a discussion about the kingdom. Jesus was going to heaven, but He said, "In my absence you are to bear witness to the transcendent, supernatural truth of my ascension." That's why our first loyalty as Christians must be to our heavenly King. We are called to respect, honor, pray for, and be in subjection to our earthly authorities, but the minute we exalt the earthly authority over the authority of Christ, we have betrayed Him, and we have committed treason against the King of kings. His authority is higher than the authority of the president of the United States or Congress or the king of Spain or any ruler anywhere else.

If you don't like the president of the United States, remember that the One who cast the deciding ballot in his election was almighty God. Of course, God doesn't sanction or endorse everything that the president does; neither is it the case that God turns the authority over to the president and says, "Go ahead and rule these people however you want." Every king is subject to the laws of God and will be judged accordingly. It may be that the president is completely ungodly, but for reasons known to God alone, God has placed him in that seat of authority.

This obviously raises the question of whether it is ever lawful to rebel against the appointed government. We will consider this question more in chapter six, but for now we should note that we ought to be wary of engaging in unlawful civil disobedience without just cause. Our fallen world is beset by evil, seen especially in lawlessness. The archenemy of the Christian faith is described as the "man of lawlessness" (2 Thess. 2:3). It was lawlessness—the sin of Adam and Eve—that plunged the world into ruin in the first place. They would not submit to the rule and reign of God. This is why I say that sin is a political matter—not in the sense of modern politics, but in the sense that God is the ultimate governor of our lives. Every time I sin, I participate in the revolt against God's perfect rule.

Paul continues in Romans 13, "Therefore whoever resists the authorities resists what God has appointed, and those who resist will incur judgment" (v. 2). Paul is obviously talking about unlawful resistance against the powers that be. In the Old Testament account of the struggle between Saul and David, we see David as a man who didn't want to unlawfully resist God's authority structures. He had many opportunities to kill Saul, but he refused to lift his hand against him. As evil as Saul was, David knew that he was God's anointed king.

When I was in seminary, I had professors who radically

denied the central truths of Christianity, things such as the atonement, the deity of Christ, and the resurrection of Jesus. They had no proper basis for being professors in a theological seminary, and I held them in disdain spiritually. But I believed it was my absolute duty in that classroom to treat them with respect. As derelict as they were, they were in the position of authority and I wasn't. That didn't mean I was supposed to believe everything they thought or slavishly accept their teaching, but from God's perspective I owed them my respect.

It is important to note that Peter and Paul do not speak of the authorities to be obeyed as necessarily being godly authorities. But they do say that God has appointed them. God raises governments up and God brings them down. The Old Testament is filled with incidents (such as that recorded in the book of Habakkuk) in which people are rebellious against God, and God punishes them by giving them wicked rulers that cause them to struggle in oppression and pain until they repent.

God as the supreme authority delegates authority for the rule of this world to His Son, Jesus Christ. Then, under Christ we have kings, parents, schoolteachers, and everyone else in authority. Thus, if I am disobedient to any authority that God has put in place, I am disobedient to Him. That's what Peter means when he says, "Be subject for the Lord's sake to every human institution" (1 Peter 2:13). We are obedient to human institutions as a means of bearing witness to the ultimate seat of cosmic authority.

Chapter Three

THE SWORD
AND THE KEYS

The Protestant Reformers believed that civil magistrates, or officials, cannot assume to themselves the administration of Word and sacrament, which are the essential duties of the church. Even in Israel, a theocratic nation, there was a distinction between the role of the priest and the role of the king.

In the Old Testament, there are only a handful of kings in Israel or Judah who were even remotely godly, among them Hezekiah, Josiah, and David. But one of the greatest kings in all of Old Testament history was Uzziah. During his reign of more than fifty years, he brought about reforms and was a man committed to godliness. However, his story is one of the most tragic in the Old Testament. Despite his righteous deeds, he died in shame, having been removed by God from the throne. Later in his life, like a Shakespearean tragedy, he committed a fatal misdeed.

What was it that he did? He went into the temple and assumed for himself the authority to administer the sacrifices. In other words, under the authority of the crown, he usurped the role of the priest, and for that, God struck him with leprosy and left him to die in disgrace and shame. We thus see that the confusion of the roles of the state and of the church dates back to ancient Israel, where the state, or more specifically, the king, took on himself the authority to control the matters that are given specifically to the church.

In order to understand the biblical separation of these two institutions, we must remember that both church and state are ordained by God. In Romans 13, the Apostle Paul states that the primary function of the state is to protect its citizens against evil. During the Reformation, Martin Luther made a distinction between the two kingdoms: the kingdom of the state and the kingdom of the church. But throughout the Middle Ages and the Reformation, the distinction between church and state was often blurred, with the state having significant authority in the affairs of the church. In this chapter, we'll consider these influences with respect to the United States, but first we'll delve more deeply into Romans 13.

In the last chapter, we considered Paul's statement: "Let every person be subject to the governing authorities. For there is no authority except from God, and those that exist have been instituted by God. Therefore whoever resists the authorities resists what God has appointed, and those who resist will incur judgment" (Rom. 13:1–2). With these strong words, Paul is instructing Christians concerning their responsibility to obey the Roman government, in spite of the fact that Rome was an extremely oppressive regime. He then goes on to say:

> For rulers are not a terror to good conduct, but to bad. Would you have no fear of the one who is in authority? Then do what is good, and you will receive his approval, for he is God's servant for your good. But if you do wrong, be afraid, for

he does not bear the sword in vain. For he is the servant of God, an avenger who carries out God's wrath on the wrongdoer. Therefore one must be in subjection, not only to avoid God's wrath but also for the sake of conscience. For because of this you also pay taxes, for the authorities are ministers of God, attending to this very thing. (vv. 3–6)

There seems to be a certain level of idealism here. The Apostle Paul was not unaware that human governments can become considerably corrupt and perpetrate gross acts of injustice, but regardless, he sets forth the appointed role of civil government as instituted by God. Government is to minister as an instrument in the hand of God to promote justice and to punish evil. Therefore, the dual concepts of law and government are intertwined in this text.

It is the function of government to enact laws, and those laws are designed to promote justice. God never gives the state the right to do wrong. The state does not exercise its authority autonomously, as a law unto itself, but is subject to the ultimate government of God Himself. For this reason, the state is held accountable by God for the promotion of justice. The spirit of what Paul says is:

"You should not live in fear of the civil magistrate, because if you are doing what is right, you will receive praise from them. You only need to fear the government if you are a transgressor. If you are engaging in wickedness, then you have something to fear from government."

Of course, this presupposes that the civil magistrate is operating in a just manner. However, we know that there are governments that will endorse, support, and uphold evil practices and principles. Historically, there have been many nations that have oppressed goodness, and in so doing have caused the righteous to suffer. But in Romans 13, Paul is not describing all governments, but rather the purpose of civil government and its responsibility before God.

To aid us in our understanding of the role of the state, Paul teaches us that the civil magistrate does not bear the sword in vain. The power of the sword represents the right of the state to use force to make its citizens comply with the law. This is why God arms the officers of the state. The first example of this was the angel with the flaming sword whom God placed at the entrance to the garden of Eden to enforce God's banishment of Adam and Eve. In like fashion, throughout history God has given the sword to the civil magistrate.

An important thing to note is that the power of the sword is not given to the church. The mission of the church does not move forward through coercion or military conflict. The emblem of Christianity is the cross. By contrast, the emblem of Islam is the scimitar or sword. In Islam, there is an agenda of conquest given to the religious authorities, but in Christianity, the church is not given the power of the sword. The power of the sword is bestowed upon the state alone.

The state's bearing the power of the sword is the biblical foundation for the classical Christian view of just war theory. Adherents to this theory would say that all wars are evil, yet not everyone's involvement in war is evil. For example, the use of the sword to protect citizens from an aggressive invasion from a hostile nation is just. In this view, an aggressive attack on innocent nations would be a violation of the state's use of the sword. A perfect example of an unjust use of the sword is the German invasion of Poland and other surrounding nations in World War II. Conversely, according to just war theory, the invaded nations were just in using the sword to repel the invaders from their territory. The point here is not to delve into all of the ramifications of warfare, but to demonstrate that this text has bearing on the issue of war since Paul speaks of God's giving the power of the sword to the civil magistrate.

It also has bearing on the controversial issue of capital punishment. God gives that power of the sword to the state, not simply to rattle the sword in its sheath, but to uphold justice and to defend the innocent and the weak from the powerful and guilty.

It is important that we understand that this power is not given to the church. The church's sphere of influence and authority is spiritual. This is ministerial power, and it is very different than the power of the sword. The saying "The pen is mightier than the sword" speaks of a greater power than physical force. In a similar way, the church has not been given the sword as the means to spread the kingdom of God, but rather the power of the Word, the power of service, and the power of imitating Christ, who did not come with a sword (Matt. 10:34).

Conversely, there is power that is given to the church alone and not to the state. The Westminster Confession of Faith expounds upon this fact in section 23.3: "Civil magistrates may not assume to themselves the administration of the Word and sacraments; or the power of the keys of the kingdom of heaven; or, in the least, interfere in matters of faith." This prohibition places certain authority in the hands of the church alone; this authority is called "the power of the keys." Jesus said to His disciples, "I will give you the keys of the kingdom of heaven, and whatever you bind on earth shall be bound in heaven, and whatever you loose on earth shall be loosed in heaven" (Matt 16:19). Jesus gave the keys of the kingdom to the church, not the state. As a result, matters of church discipline are not the state's business.

In the United States, there have been occasions in recent years when churches have disciplined members and the member being disciplined has attempted to appeal the ecclesiastical decision in a civil court. Unfortunately, there have been cases as well where the civil court has overturned the church's decision to excommunicate the unrepentant sinner. This is a clear usurpation of the ecclesiastical role by the civil magistrate.

In the United States, the First Amendment guarantees the church the right to free exercise of religion without interference by the civil magistrate. However, when the civil magistrate assumes the power of the keys, it not only stands in defiance of the First Amendment, but, more importantly, it stands in defiance of God.

The Westminster Confession goes on: "Yet, as nursing

fathers, it is the duty of civil magistrates to protect the church of our common Lord, without giving the preference to any denomination of Christians above the rest, in such a manner that all ecclesiastical persons shall enjoy the full, free, and unquestioned liberty of discharging every part of their sacred functions, without violence or danger" (23.3). The need for a clear division of labor between the church and the state was a principle that emerged out of the Protestant Reformation. The church was called to pray for the state and to be supportive of the state. The state was called to guarantee the liberty of the church and protect the church from those that would seek to destroy it. There was to be no favoritism to any particular denomination or group of believers. This is the root of the principle of separation of church and state.

Continuing on in the Westminster Confession: "And, as Jesus Christ hath appointed a regular government and discipline in his church, no law of any commonwealth should interfere with, let, or hinder the due exercise thereof, among the voluntary members of *any* denomination of Christians, according to their own profession and belief" (23.3, emphasis original). Churches should have courts, and the church court is to function without interference from the civil court. The two are to remain distinct and to respect each other's jurisdictions.

As we struggle with the question of the relationship of church and state in our time, it's difficult to remain objective. We all are products of our individual cultural contexts. As Christians, we need to form our viewpoints from the Word of God, so that we gain a clear understanding of how the church is supposed to function, what its mission is, and how that mission is different from the role of government.

The church is called to be a critic of the state when the state fails to obey its mandate under God. For example, in the controversy over abortion, when the church is critical of the state with respect to the idea of abortion, people are angered and say, "The church is trying to impose its agenda on the state." However, the primary reason that government exists is to protect, maintain, and support human life. When the church complains about the abortion laws in America, the church is not asking the state to be the church. The church is asking the state to be the state. It is simply asking the state to do its God-ordained job.

Chapter Four

Established
Religion

Among the longest words in the English language is *antidisestablishmentarianism*. However, this word is not merely a bit of trivia; it is key to understanding the relationship between church and state.

Let's take a look at what the word means. It is a double negative: it refers to the view that is against *disestablishmentarianism*, which in turn is against *establishmentarianism*. Establishmentarianism is when a church is supported by taxes from the state and has exclusive rights over its competitors. Such a church, called an *established* church, enjoys the particular favor and protection of the government; historical examples include the Church of England, the Lutheran church in Germany, the Reformed church of Scotland, or the Swedish Lutheran church. Disestablishmentarians believe that establishmentarianism should be repudiated. Antidisestablishmentarianism—the double negative makes it a positive—means that you're opposed to disestablishing a church. This view looks with favor on an established church.

If you consider American history, you can quickly understand why the United States does not have an established state church. It was customary in sixteenth- and seventeenth-century Europe to have an established church. States were either officially Roman Catholic or some form of Protestant. England became Protestant under Henry VIII in the seventeenth century. Henry wanted to get a divorce and the pope wouldn't allow it, so Henry declared himself free from Roman Catholic authority. When Henry declared himself and his country free from Rome's authority, he gave himself the title *defensor fide*, or "defender of the faith." The crown was then seen as sovereign not only in the civil arena, but also in ecclesiastical matters. This would have radical consequences for future generations in England.

Despite breaking away from the Roman Catholic Church, Henry was not all that Protestant in his theological perspective. When he died, he was succeeded by Edward VI. He was self-consciously Protestant and sought to bring the Church of England into a fully Protestant and Reformed understanding of Christianity. But his reign was very short, and when he died at an early age, he was succeeded by his sister Mary.

Queen Mary I is better known as Bloody Mary. She received this title because she brought England back to the Roman Catholic Church via an extensive program of persecution against Protestants. This led to the many martyrdoms of the English Reformation. Many were burned at the stake through the decrees of Bloody Mary. Numerous leaders of England's Protestant Reformation movement fled into exile, often to Germany or Switzerland. The Geneva Bible was written by English exiles in Switzerland in the middle of the sixteenth century during the reign of Bloody Mary. It was the dominant English Bible for a hundred years.

When Mary passed from the scene, her half-sister, Elizabeth, replaced her. Queen Elizabeth I became known as Good Queen Bess or the Virgin Queen. She restored England to Protestantism and welcomed the return of the refugees who had fled from the persecution of her sister, Mary. Oftentimes, we think of Queen Elizabeth as the benign, compassionate queen who put an end to the bloody persecutions. This is not so. One would think that she would have made Roman Catholics the object of her persecution, but that was not the case either. Rather, she carried out an extensive campaign of persecution against certain Protestants within her realm. These Protestants were called Nonconformists because they were not satisfied with the established Church of England.

The Nonconformists believed that the Anglican Church under Queen Elizabeth was not Reformed enough and had retained too many practices reminiscent of the Roman Catholic style of worship. Stylistic elements included the rituals of the Lord's Supper and the garments of the priests. In addition, the Nonconformists protested against the requirement to wear the white surplices of the priesthood during the celebration of worship. They believed this was objectionable because it confused the common people, who saw these vestments as a symbol of the Roman Catholicism they had rejected. Nonetheless, Queen Elizabeth passed legislation requiring the Nonconformists to wear the surplice. As a result, many ministers of the Church of England resisted and were removed from their positions. Some were thrown into prison and some were executed by the queen. These Nonconformists became known by the pejorative word *Puritan*.

These Puritans sought relief from persecution by fleeing to other countries for refuge. Many fled to the Netherlands and many others came to the United States. As a result, places such as New England and Virginia have a strong heritage of dislike for governmental interference in church matters. But people fled to America not only from England, but also from other countries in Europe, both Protestant countries and Catholic countries. At this time in history, Protestants were persecuting Catholics and Catholics were persecuting Protestants.

In light of this cultural context, it's easy to see why the United States was founded as a place were religious freedom and toleration would reign. This is the principle of non-establishmentarianism. It declares that there will be no state church. It was designed to protect the rights of religious people to practice their religion without interference and without prejudice at the hands of the civil magistrate. It's easy to understand, then, why the First Amendment of the U.S. Constitution guarantees the free exercise of religion. Protestants had to live in peace with Catholics and Catholics with Protestants. People of all religions—whether they were Jews, Muslims, Hindus, Buddhists, or Christians—were equally tolerated under the law.

One of the unfortunate consequences of this foundational principle is the common assumption that all religions are not just tolerated but are equally true and valid. However, the government has no right to make these claims. The law does not declare who is right and who is wrong. All it says is that those disputes should not be dealt with in the civil arena. Instead, those are religious and ecclesiastical matters and are to remain outside of the scope and the sphere of civil government.

Christians need to be very careful about trying to persuade the civil magistrate to take up their agenda. The United States is a nation in which we are supposed to be committed to the principle of separation and division of labors.

On the other hand, in today's culture, separation of

church and state has come to mean that the government rules without taking God into consideration. That is not the way this nation was founded. I certainly don't believe this country was founded by a monolithically Christian body. I believe the Mayflower Compact of the seventeenth century was monolithically Christian, but not the Constitution or Declaration of Independence. There were many Christians and non-Christians involved, but it was clearly theistic. That is, the United States was founded on the principle of both church and state being under God. But today, we hate the concept of being answerable to God. We want to have a government that is free from the moral taint of theism. That's not the original intent of the First Amendment or of the original articles that established our nation.

Our forefathers sought to keep the state out of religious matters, but today, the thing they wanted to avoid is happening. There are many examples of intrusion by the state into the life of the church. It is happening in very subtle ways, but it is happening nonetheless. It happens with zoning laws and it happens with restrictions placed upon church buildings and how large they can be, or how high their steeples can be. It is happening in reference to gay marriage and whether churches have a right to refuse wedding services to gay couples. In addition, employers are being asked to provide medical coverage for employees that includes coverage for abortion.

I believe we're going to see more and more of these collisions between the secular state and the church as we move into the future. World history is full of examples of governments oppressing the church of Christ. We shouldn't be all that surprised. We should resist where we are able, but we should also rest in the sovereignty of God. He will build His church, and His kingdom is forever.

It's easy for us to take for granted the freedoms we do have in the United States. But we should be quick to remember the price that was paid for those freedoms. May we recall the historical circumstances of our forefathers who fled from the worst kinds of persecution at the hands of civil governments. Because people were not willing to embrace the established church, the state used the sword to impose a particular creed upon the people. This was patently wrong. It was wrong for them, and it would be wrong for us if we were ever to attempt the same thing.

The kingdom of God is not built by an edict from an

emperor or the might of an army. It is built through one means alone: the proclamation of the gospel. That's the power that God has ordained to build His church—not the power of the sword—and as Christians, we will continue to place our hope in this power and this power alone.

Chapter Five

An Instrument
of Evil

Christians in America sometimes have a tendency to mingle their religious devotion with a brand of super-patriotism. Some wrap our national flag in the banner of Christ, assuming that God is always on our side. However, no matter where we live, our first allegiance is to our King and to the heavenly kingdom to which we belong. And further, we have to understand that whether it's Germany,

Babylon, Rome, Russia, or the United States, any government can be corrupted.

As we continue to study the relationship between church and state, we must consider an aspect of that relationship which is mainly ignored and somewhat difficult to comprehend. Ephesians 6:10 is a familiar passage to many of us, but few ever apply it to the relationship of church and state. Paul writes:

> Finally, be strong in the Lord and in the strength of his might. Put on the whole armor of God, that you may be able to stand against the schemes of the devil. For we do not wrestle against flesh and blood, but against the rulers, against the authorities, against the cosmic powers over this present darkness, against the spiritual forces of evil in the heavenly places. Therefore take up the whole armor of God, that you may be able to withstand in the evil day, and having done all, to stand firm. (Eph. 6:10–13)

This famous passage concerning the armor of God is given to us by the Apostle Paul in order to encourage

Christians to stand against the craftiness of Satan. This may seem somewhat strange today, since there is little attention given to the realm of the satanic. It is common now to completely dismiss Satan from our consciousness.

But to Paul, the realm of the satanic was very real. When he talks about putting on the armor of God, he's telling us to be girded for spiritual battle. It's not a battle against flesh and blood, but it is a battle against spiritual forces. Paul identifies them as rulers and authorities and as spiritual forces of evil in the heavenly places. He's telling us to become equipped to engage in spiritual conflict that involves the rulers of some kind of spiritual, hidden realm.

In the New Testament, the power, oppression, and tyranny of Rome are a recurring theme. For example, much of the eschatological vision in the book of Revelation is written to people experiencing persecution from the Romans. Most Christians think the Beast described in Revelation is referring to some future, earthly governor. But there are also serious scholars who believe that the primary reference of the beast is to Nero. He was the incarnation of wickedness in Roman history, and his nickname throughout the Roman empire was, oddly enough, "the Beast." While it is disputed whether he was the one who is specifically in view in the book of Revelation, I mainly want to demonstrate that human governments can become instruments of spiritual powers and principalities that unleash all kinds of evil into the world.

Recent history has provided numerous painful examples of the demonization of the state. World War II provided a front-row seat to an unprecedented form of inhuman behavior in Hitler's Third Reich. Hitler's Nazi regime murdered millions, and he was followed by the atheistic regimes of Joseph Stalin's Soviet Union, Mao Zedong's China, and Pol Pot's Khmer Rouge. How can governments become so corrupt that they actually become tools in the hand of satanic powers? First, we've established that the primary function of the government, as ordained by God, is to protect, sustain, and maintain the sanctity of human life. When governments engage in genocide, such as we saw in Germany, in Soviet Russia, or in Iraq, those governments become servants of the Enemy because they destroy human life without just cause.

An example of the state's failing to project the sanctity of human life is the modern-day scourge of on-demand abortion. Hundreds and thousands of unborn babies are destroyed under the sanction of the government every year.

When the church protests against this injustice, it is not trying to intrude into the domain of the state. It is simply reminding the state that its primary function is to protect life. Any government that sanctions the destruction of life has failed in its divine mandate to govern.

Second, governments are instituted to protect private property. Two of the Ten Commandments specifically protect the rights of individuals to the property they possess. When private property is not protected by or is confiscated by the government, the government abuses its right to rule by using its power to legalize the theft of people's private property. For example, in the Old Testament, when King Ahab confiscated Naboth's vineyard, the prophet Elijah pronounced the judgment of God upon him.

Recall the warning given to the people of Israel when they asked to have a king like the other nations. They didn't want God to be their king; they wanted kings whom they could see with their eyes. God warned them that this king would go to war and take their children for his army. He would take their horses and fields and confiscate their property. He would burden them with unjust taxation (1 Sam. 8:10–18). And that is exactly what their kings did, and what rulers have done throughout world history.

As we see in Romans 13, God gives governments a legitimate right to tax their people to pay for the necessities of government, and Christians are called to pay their taxes. However, governments can become greedy and unjust in their taxation programs by mandating tax laws that are essentially confiscation.

One of the speakers at a national political convention discussed the dream of wealth redistribution. This is the socialist dream that says we should spread out the wealth of the country so we have everyone comfortably in the middle class. This is all done in the name of economic equality. You take from those who have more and give to those who have less. From each according to his ability; to each according to his need. In a classroom setting, it would be like taking someone who had earned an A and taking someone else who had earned a D, then giving them both C's, along with the rest of the class. It wouldn't matter how they performed on tests, how well they studied, or how they prepared or labored. Everyone would receive the same grade. Supposedly, that's equality. But it's not. Equality is not the same thing as equity, and this kind of distributive policy violates the very role God gave government, namely, to protect people's private property.

When governments take the possessions of their people, they try to justify it by appeal to some higher goal or destiny. But no one has the right to do what is wrong, even if they are appealing to a greater good. For instance, it is still stealing if I take from you to give to someone else, even if I do it with my vote. We call that entitlement. But I am not entitled to your property, nor am I entitled to steal from you. It doesn't matter what my intentions are or if my stealing is limited to taking from the rich. However, in our culture today, it's considered acceptable to take from the rich because "they can afford it."

As Christians, it is important that we don't practice this kind of political activity. We don't want to become a part of a system where you can use the ballot to enrich yourself for your own interests. Unfortunately, in the United States, special-interest groups devoted to wealth redistribution are not only tolerated but welcomed in the nation's capital. As we've seen in God's Word, we are prohibited from using political clout to take from others to enrich ourselves. As a result, we should not participate in government-sanctioned stealing.

Chapter Six

CIVIL
DISOBEDIENCE

A wonderful lesson about the Christian's responsibility before the state can be found in a surprising place in the Bible.

You might be familiar with the Christmas story in Luke 2. The story opens by noting an edict by Augustus Caesar. As part of his taxation program, Caesar commanded everyone to return to their city of birth so that they could be counted in the census. As a result, people were subjected to all kinds of hardships. Many had to make arduous journeys in order to satisfy Caesar's demand for taxation. They were not returning to their roots for a vacation, but rather to be in submission to the governing authority.

Because of that decree, Joseph and Mary undertook the long journey from Nazareth in Galilee to Bethlehem. Joseph could have protested, saying, "Wait a minute. My wife is nine months pregnant, and if I subject her to this journey to Bethlehem in order to sign up for the census, I could lose my wife and our unborn child." He could have made a great case for the injustice of the law, and he could have simply refused to obey it.

But that's not what he did. He risked the life of his wife and baby to be in compliance with the law even though the law was a great inconvenience to them.

Joseph's example raises an important issue—that of civil disobedience. Is there ever a time when it is legitimate for the church or the Christian to act in defiance toward the state? This has been a highly controversial matter since the founding of the United States. Many Christians were divided on whether it was legitimate to declare independence from the crown of England. The issues are rather complex, and there is much disagreement among

Christian theologians and ethicists when it comes to civil disobedience.

When Paul wrote, "Let every person be subject to the governing authorities" (Rom. 13:1), he was writing to people who were suffering under the oppression of the Roman government. Yet, Paul taught the believers in Rome to be good subjects of the empire, to pay their taxes, to give honor to the authorities over them, and to pray regularly for those who were in positions of power and authority (v. 7).

The Westminster Confession of Faith says, "It is the duty of people to pray for magistrates, to honor their persons, to pay them tribute or other dues, to obey their lawful commands, and to be subject to their authority, for conscience' sake. Infidelity, or difference in religion, does not make void the magistrates' just and legal authority, nor free the people from their due obedience to them" (23.4). This means that if the state is irreligious and differs from us in terms of our religious convictions, we are not freed from our responsibility to honor it as the government. We continue to pray for our government officials and pay taxes. This is our calling, even if we disagree with how we are taxed and how tax revenue is spent by the government.

Therefore, the first principle is civil *obedience*. The

principle of civil obedience is that we are called to be in submission to authorities ruling over us—and not only when we agree with them. Indeed, Christians are called to be model citizens.

This was the defense of the Christian apologists of the first and second centuries when persecution arose in the Roman Empire against them. For example, Justin Martyr defended himself and others to Emperor Antoninus Pius, by saying that Christians were the empire's most loyal citizens, commanded by King Jesus to honor the emperor. Justin understood the ethic of civil obedience that is deeply rooted in the New Testament. In fact, the ethic is so often repeated in Scripture that one could easily come to the conclusion that we must always obey the civil magistrate. As we will see, this is not the case, but the overwhelming emphasis in Scripture is that Christians should seek to be obedient to the government whenever possible.

Does that mean we must always obey? Absolutely not. There are times when Christians are free to disobey the magistrate, but there are also times when we *must* disobey the civil magistrate. Consider an episode from the book of Acts when Peter and John were called before the Sanhedrin, the rulers of the Jews, after healing a crippled man:

Now when they saw the boldness of Peter and John, and perceived that they were uneducated, common men, they were astonished. And they recognized that they had been with Jesus. But seeing the man who was healed standing beside them, they had nothing to say in opposition. But when they had commanded them to leave the council, they conferred with one another, saying, "What shall we do with these men? For that a notable sign has been performed through them is evident to all the inhabitants of Jerusalem, and we cannot deny it. But in order that it may spread no further among the people, let us warn them to speak no more to anyone in this name." (Acts 4:13–17)

By the power of Christ, Peter and John had healed the man that was crippled. The Jewish leaders knew that is was a miracle from God but understood the implications of acknowledging that fact. One would think they would have said, "Therefore, since this miracle was performed right in front of our eyes by the power of Christ, we ought to repent and subject ourselves to Him." That's what they should have said, but instead they said: "We can't deny this. But we can slow the growth of this sect that we abhor with their miracles. Let us severely threaten them, that from now on they speak to no man in this name. Let us use the power and authority that we have as rulers over them to give severe threats against them, to put a stop to their preaching in the name of Christ."

What happened? "So they called them and charged them not to speak or teach at all in the name of Jesus" (v. 18).

It is important to pause and reflect on what the Jewish leaders were doing. The authorities commanded Peter and John never to speak or teach about Christ again. In light of that, consider this: Would you be reading this book right now if Peter and John had obeyed that mandate? Had the Apostolic community submitted to the authorities and became subject to that mandate, Christianity would have ended right then and there.

But what happened was very plain. The magistrate commanded them to be quiet, prohibiting them from doing what Christ had commanded them to do. In response, consider the principle that emerges in the next verses: "But Peter and John answered them, 'Whether it is right in the sight of God to listen to you rather than to God, you must judge, for we cannot but speak of what we have seen and heard'" (vv. 19–20).

Whom do you obey when there is a direct, immediate, and unequivocal conflict between the law of God and the rule of men? At times, human rulers require people to do things that God forbids, or forbids them from doing what God commands. The principle is very simple. If any ruler—a governing official or body, school teacher, boss, or military commander—commands you to do something God forbids or forbids you from doing something God commands, not only *may* you disobey, but you *must* disobey. If it comes down to a choice like this, you must obey God.

You can memorize this principle in a few moments, but the application can be exceedingly complex. As sinful people, we must realize that we are very prone to twist and distort things in our favor in order to benefit ourselves. Before we disobey the authorities over us, we should be sure to be painfully self-reflective and have a clear understanding as to *why* we plan to disobey.

If my boss told me to cook the books so that he could be protected from the charge of embezzlement, I would have to disobey. If a governmental authority told you that you had to have an abortion, you would have to disobey because you obey a higher authority. If the authorities say we're not allowed to distribute Bibles or preach the Word of God, we have to do it anyway because we have a mandate from Christ to disciple the nations.

This is why the free exercise of religion is so important. It gives the right to act according to conscience, but unfortunately, this right is currently being eroded in the United States.

When I was teaching at a university during the Vietnam War, I had many students in my classes who were opposed to the war. They sought to opt out of involvement in the war through conscientious objection. They asked me if I would sign affidavits to verify that they truly held this objection, and I did. I signed several of these documents, but not because I thought the students had a good understanding of the complexities of the war, nor because I was convinced that America was wrong for being there. In fact, I wasn't sure whether we should have been there. But these young people *were* sure that our involvement was wrong. I was simply testifying that they were sincere.

At that time in history, so many young people sought conscientious objector status that it became a crisis. In response, the government changed the regulations such that you could only receive the status of a contentious objector if you could prove that you were opposed to *all* wars, not simply that particular one. In other words, you had to be a certifiable pacifist. But for many Christians throughout history, such a black-and-white approach to war would be too simplistic and would put many believers in a very challenging position in regard to civil disobedience.

While the principle of conscience has eroded in our government, acts of civil disobedience have remained. This was demonstrated in the civil rights movement of the mid-twentieth century, when large groups of oppressed people transgressed local statutes. This movement sought to make it plain that local laws were unjust and violated the Constitution of the United States.

Because the matter of civil disobedience is complicated, it's vitally important that we master the basic principles regarding the relationship between church and state. As Paul says in Romans 13, we are to be subject to the authorities that are placed over us, because their power is a derivative power, given to them by God Himself. This is the principle of civil obedience. But when those authorities command us to do something God forbids or forbid us from doing something God commands, we must obey God rather than earthly authorities.

God has established two realms on earth: the church

and the state. Each one has its own sphere of authority, and neither is to infringe on the rights of the other. And as Christians, we are to show great respect and concern for them both.

About the Author

Dr. R.C. Sproul is the founder and chairman of Ligonier Ministries, an international Christian discipleship organization located near Orlando, Fla. He also serves as copastor at Saint Andrew's Chapel in Sanford, Fla., as chancellor of Reformation Bible College, and as executive editor of *Tabletalk* magazine. His teaching can be heard around the world on the daily radio program *Renewing Your Mind*.

During his distinguished academic career, Dr. Sproul helped train men for the ministry as a professor at several theological seminaries.

He is author of more than ninety books, including *The Holiness of God*, *Chosen by God*, *The Invisible Hand*, *Faith Alone*, *Everyone's a Theologian*, *Truths We Confess*, *The Truth of the Cross*, and *The Prayer of the Lord*. He also served as general editor of the *Reformation Study Bible* and has written several children's books, including *The Donkey Who Carried a King*. Dr. Sproul and his wife, Vesta, make their home in Sanford, Fla.

Further your Bible study with *Tabletalk* magazine, another learning tool from R.C. Sproul.

....

TABLETALK MAGAZINE FEATURES:

- A Bible study for each day—bringing the best in biblical scholarship together with down-to-earth writing, *Tabletalk* helps you understand the Bible and apply it to daily living.

- Trusted theological resource—*Tabletalk* avoids trends, shallow doctrine and popular movements to present biblical truth simply and clearly.

- Thought-provoking topics—each issue contains challenging, stimulating articles on a wide variety of topics related to theology and Christian living.

Sign up for a free 3-month trial of *Tabletalk* magazine and we will send you R.C. Sproul's *The Holiness of God*

TryTabletalk.com/CQ